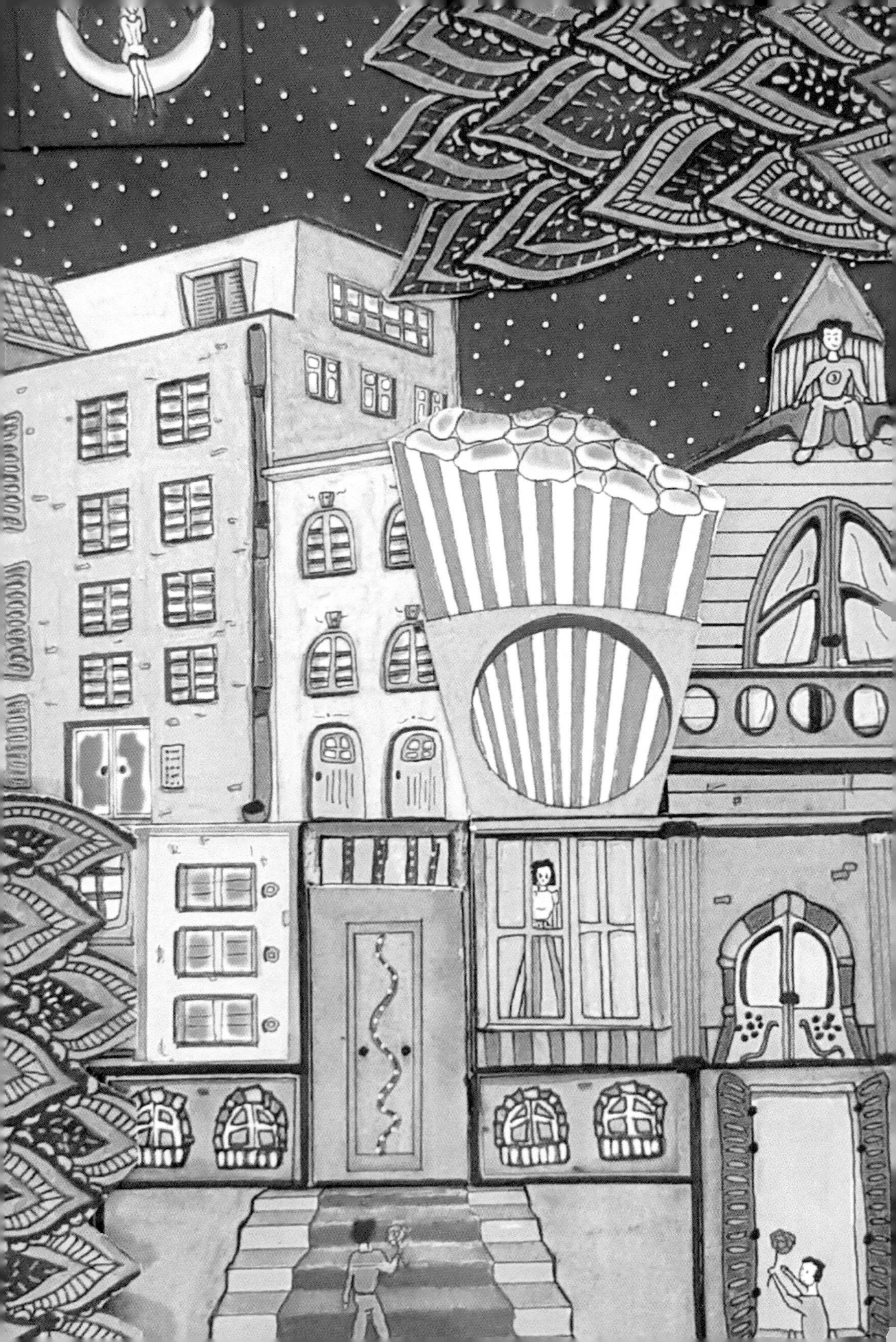

Rose Dollsweet

Presents

VICTORIA
EAST

Canada

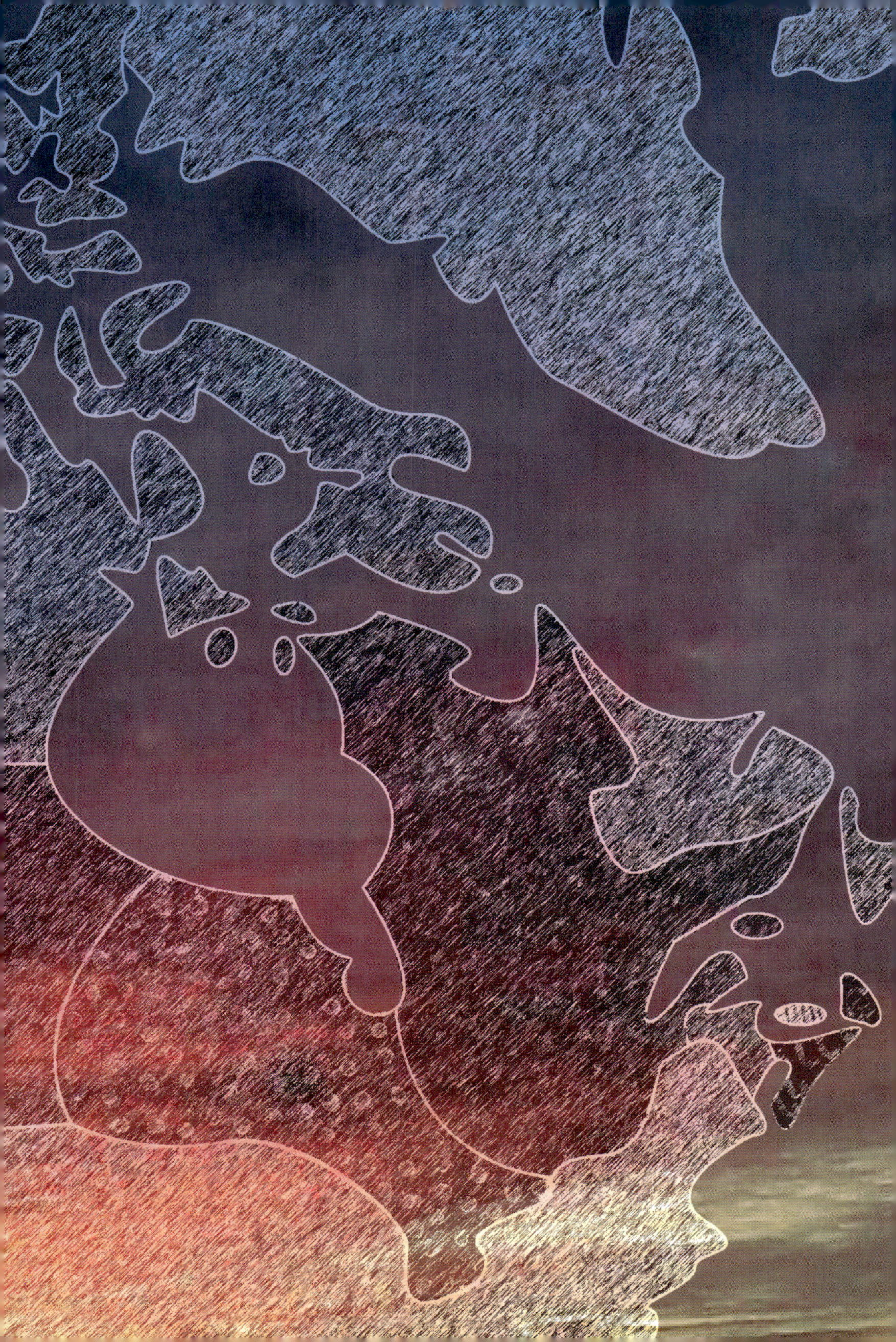

Travel Victoria Collection

'Travel Victoria' is a collection of travel guide books created in 2021 with its first release 'Victoria Center' and continuing in 2022 with 'Victoria East'. It comes along with a new map of Victoria and its surroundings designed to facilitate the adventures around this beautiful capital and this incredible island. Across these books, you will be immersed inside of the wonderful parks, beaches, activities, and amazing surprises that this destination has to offer.

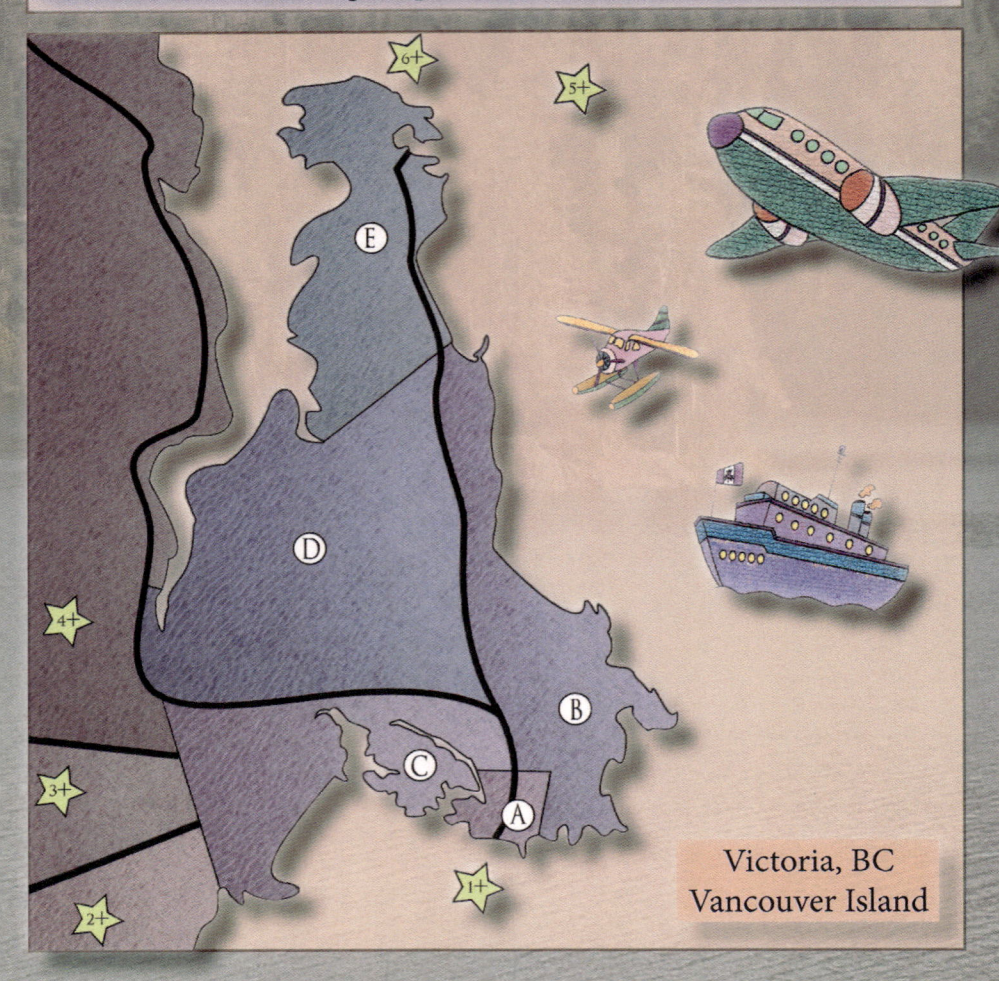

Victoria, BC
Vancouver Island

Victoria City

Catch a ferry or seaplane from the northeast Pacific ocean to come to Vancouver Island! The largest island on the west coast of North America with 460 km of exceptional nature and wildlife! Mostly made up of volcanic and sedimentary rock, this island has become one of the best destinations in British Columbia. On the island, there is Victoria city, the elegant and beautiful capital of British Columbia since 1871 that boasts a british life style! Victoria is a happy and relaxing place and also one of the oldest cities in the Pacific Northwest that has retained a large number of its historic buildings! It is one of the most cute and lovely cities surrounded by the ocean, lakes, regional parks, and so many activities to enjoy in any season! The map on the left was specifically divided and labeled for the collection 'Travel Victoria' for you to travel and explore easily around the city. The different parts have been split into 5 books for the collection plus 1 bonus book for the outskirts. For your enjoyment, Travel Victoria present its second book, 'Victoria East'.

- Welcome to Victoria BC -

This book is a rare travel book that will take you into the complete universe of the east side of Victoria BC! Published in the interest of helping and simplifying your adventures!

Victoria East

- Welcome to Victoria East -

BEST OF BEACHES

Best of Beaches Map	p2
Willows Beach	p3
Cadboro-Gyro Beach	p4
Arbutus Cove Beach	p5
Cormorant Point Beach	p6
Mount Douglas Beach	p7
McMorran Beach	p8
Agate Beach	p9
Parker Beach	p10
Island View Beach	p11
Saanichton Bay	p12

OCEAN SIDE

Ocean Side Map	p16
Little Ross Bay Beach	p17
Public Beach Access	p18
Gonzales Bay	p19
Trafalgar Park	p20
McNeill Bay	p21
Turkey Head Walkway	p22
Cattle Point	p23
Funnel Cove Beach	p24
Spoon Bay Beach	p25
Loon Bay Beach	p26
Hibbens Close Beach	p27
Baynes Beach	p28
Telegraph Cove Beach	p29
Cranford & Guinevere	p30
Finnerty Cove Beach	p31
Hollydene Beach	p32
Glencoe Cove Kwatsech	p33
Ocean Staircases	p34

Victoria East

- Welcome to Victoria East -

PARKS & GARDENS

Parks & Gardens Map	p38
Abkhazi Garden	p39
Walbran Park	p40
Gonzales Hill	p41
Anderson Hill Park	p42
Bowker Creek Walkway	p43
Carnarvon Park	p44
Upland park	p45
Mount Tolmie	p46
Cedar Hill Park	p47
Finnerty Garden	p48
Mystic Vale	p49
Phyllis Park	p50
Konukson Park	p51
Haro Woods Park	p52
Bow Park	p53
Swan Lake	p54
Blenkinsop Lake	p55
Mount Douglas	p56

ACTIVITIES

Activities Map	p60
University of Victoria	p61
Ice Skating & Hockey	p62
Rec Centers & Spas	p63
Cafés, Teas & Gelatos	p64
Restaurants & Pubs	p65
Shopping Centers	p66
Uptown Area	p67
Oak Bay Avenue	p68
4Cats Art Studio	p69
Arts Alive Oak Bay	p70
Oak Bay Beach Hotel	p71
Kayaking & Paddling	p72
Biking & Riding	p73
Tennis & Golf	p74
City Parks	p75
Autumn/Winter Walks	p76
Spring/Summer Walks	p77
Wildlife & Sealife	p78

Map Victoria East

Legend Map East

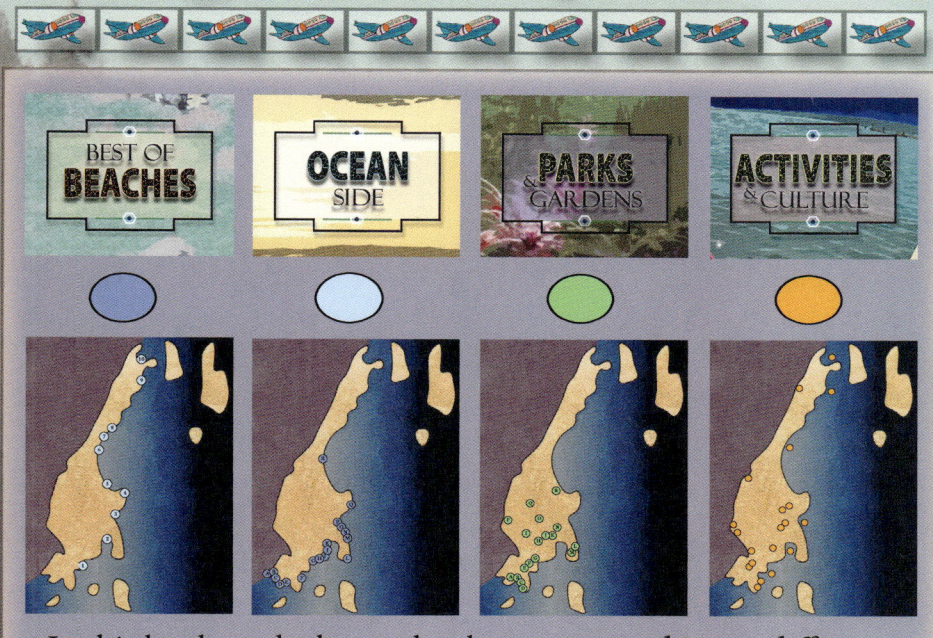

BEST OF BEACHES | **OCEAN SIDE** | **PARKS & GARDENS** | **ACTIVITIES & CULTURE**

In this book, each chapter has been separated into 4 different themes represented by colored circles on the maps throughout the book. Each location has a recommended minimun time to enjoy all it has to offer based on the author's experience.

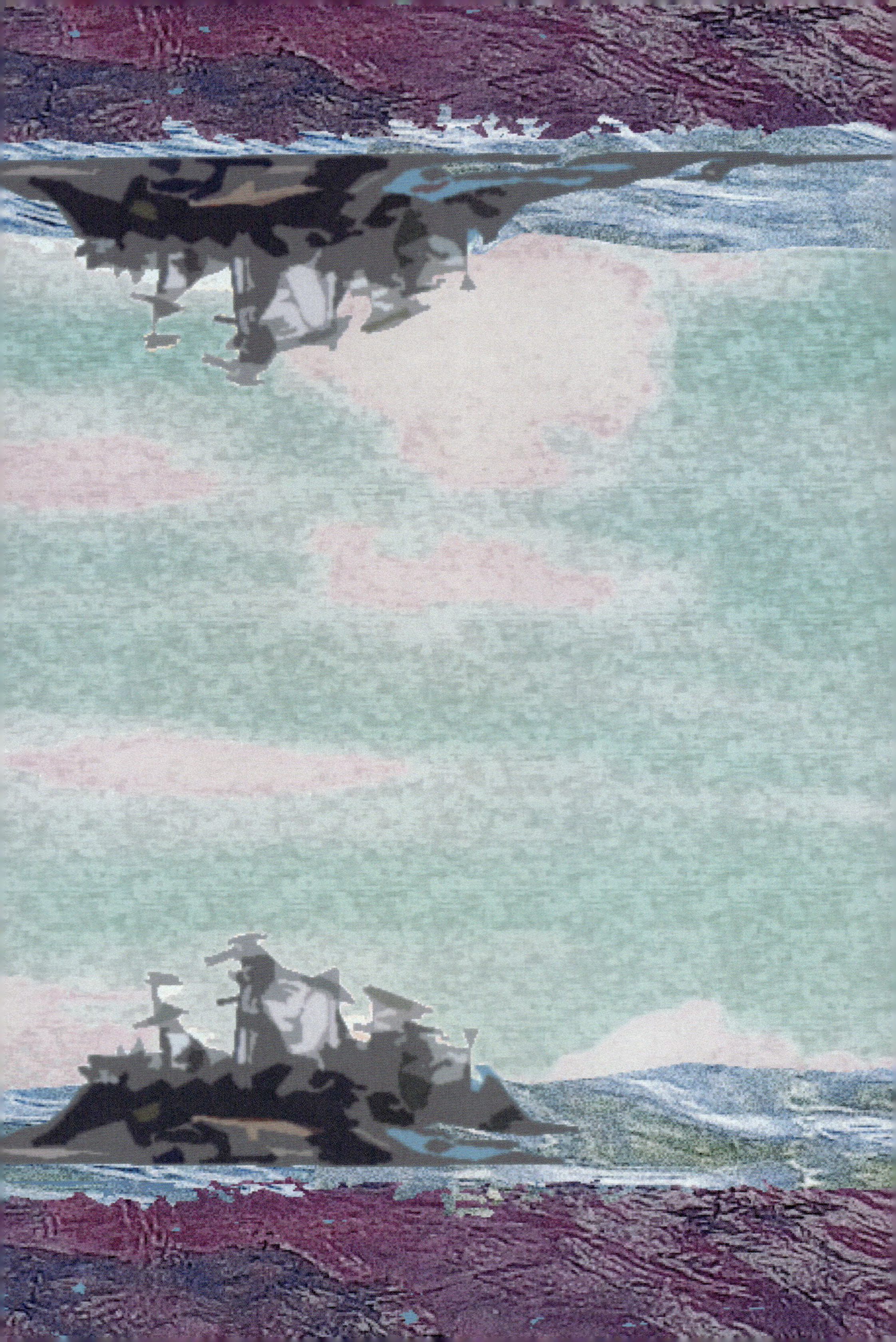

BEST OF
BEACHES

2

1 WILLOWS BEACH

**IDEAL TIME
1 – 3 HOURS
DAY/NIGHT**

Willows Beach is one of the prettiest and sandy beaches of the city. It is the perfect place to go swimming, kayaking and paddle boarding all year round. Unfortunately, during the warmer weather, the water gets less and less clear due to the seaweed and the geese, but it is still nice to go. There you will discover the beach and its nice stretch of sand covered with driftwood and right next to it is a wide grass field. It is ideal for a picnic or sports games and one of the best places for the warm evenings of summer. Furthermore, you will find a tea room where you can enjoy drinks and snacks during the day and a few steps away, there are many other cafés and restaurants.

DAY & NIGHT

2 CADBORO-GYRO BEACH

IDEAL TIME 1 – 3 HOURS DAY/NIGHT

Cadboro-Gryo is a very alluring, sandy beach that is well known and is perfect to enjoy the warm summer evenings. The water is also clearest during the winter like Willows Beach and it is one of the most perfect places to go for swimming and scuba diving all year. For the children, there is a nice area filled with playground equipment in the shapes of sea monsters with a few picnic tables around. This is an ideal spot for family fun where people come to relax, walk, or play anytime. While the place is superb, it can become very windy. Nearby there are a few cafés, patisseries, and a little supermarket perfect for your afternoon snack.

DAY & NIGHT

4

3 ARBUTUS COVE PARK / BEACH

**IDEAL TIME
1 HOUR
DAY**

Arbutus Cove, although small, is a charming park with so many varieties of lovely and beautiful ocean views in any direction you choose. This area is really calm, peaceful, and full of greenery with some very pretty houses on one side and nice tall trees on the other. There are two main access points to the beach. The first access is the busiest with a descent leading to a lovely sandy beach where you can find some shells and enjoy a longer walk. The second access is on the left side of the park and starts with a little narrow passage leading to a small, rock-covered beach where you will find a sublime view and super clear water.

DAY

4 CORMORANT POINT BEACH

IDEAL TIME
30 MIN-1 HOUR
DAY/SUNSET

Cormorant Point is a great beach in a quiet area where you can meet many little deer during your visit. Here you can enjoy a walk on a stretch of sand and gravel, dip your feet into the water, or have a picnic while you linger to catch the sumptuous sunset that goes from yellow to red. At the end of the beach, you will find some rocks on which you can climb on to admire a magnificent view and venture directly to the beginning of Mount Douglas Beach. Around this area, charming little natural pools form during the winter but sadly, during the summer this water evaporates. As a bonus, you will have a chance to see some lovely sea otters over there.

SUNSET

5 MOUNT DOUGLAS BEACH

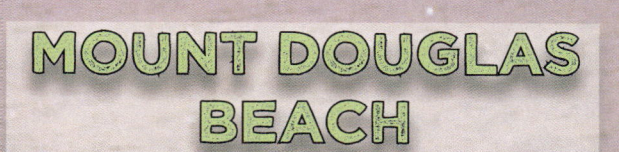

IDEAL TIME
1 - 2 HOURS
DAY

The best thing to do at Mt. Douglas Beach is to enjoy a wonderful walk along the original and wide stretch of sand. It has large rocks protruding from all over the sand and into the water. The view is amazing and the place is really peaceful. You can start this walk directly between the rocks after the view point from Cormorant, then, from there you can have a chance to see quite a few animals if you watch carefully. Between trees, rocks, sea creatures, and shells, you will feel like you are in a small paradise of nature. Be careful and watch out for the rising tide which varies throughout the day, especially because there are not many public exits.

DAY

7

6 MCMORRAN BEACH ACCESS

**IDEAL TIME
1 – 4 HOURS
DAY/NIGHT**

McMorran Beach is probably the most popular access to the lovely Cordova Bay. It is a stunning beach of fine sand and clear water which makes it ideal for swimming during the summer heat, even if the water is always a bit chilly. Its amazing moonlight stands out the most across the entire bay which you can also admire from the patio of the Beach House restaurant with its breathtaking view of the ocean. There you can enjoy a cocktail or a romantic dinner at sunset. You can also walk around the neighbourhood, where you will find many luxury homes, each as gorgeous as the other and have a chance to see many deer eating in the beautiful gardens.

DAY & NIGHT

8

7 — AGATE PARK / BEACH

IDEAL TIME
30 MIN-1 HOUR
DAY

Agate Park is a nice little green space with stunning oceanviews and easy access to one of Cordova Bay's sandy beaches. To the left of this beach, there is a nice dog friendly beach and Maycock Point beach which follow each other through the golden sand. The water is super clear all year round which is ideal for swimming or relaxing on your buoy. It is also a great place to enjoy a walk during a beautiful sunny day or an early evening moonlight stroll. You will also find a handmade rope swing hanging from the big tree trunk at the entrance. Here you can enjoy the infinite horizon and beautiful mountain landscape.

DAY

9

8 PARKER PARK / BEACH

IDEAL TIME
1 HOUR
DAY

The beach of Parker park is one of the most magnificent, atypical, and brilliant beaches of Cordova Bay. You will be surrounded by a pleasant and warming feeling of nature as you walk along the tall trees on the sandy beach. It is one of the best places to swim and soak up the beautiful view. It feels like a super adventure that takes you to an exciting world away from reality. At the end, just before Sayward Beach, you will see a rocky area that is easy to climb for an even greater view of the sky and ocean. It is best enjoyed under a bright sunny sun. In the distance, you can see an old wooden staircase reinforcing the original look, even if you can not use it.

10

9 ISLAND VIEW BEACH

**IDEAL TIME
1 - 3 HOURS
DAY**

Island View is a very long beach that has a mix of sand and small rocks along the shore. This place is even more isolated than all the other beaches of the east. It has an amazing and attractive water with a magnificent landscape in the background. It is nice to soak your feet or enjoy a summer swim, even though the water remains cold. You can also relax on your beach chair or one of the many driftwood logs. At the edge of the beach there is a large regional park with several different small trails in which you can continue your walk for a long time. A hat and plenty of water are highly recommended as the heat can be very strong here.

DAY

11

10 SAANICHTON BAY

**IDEAL TIME
1 – 3 HOUR
DAY**

Saanichton Bay is a beautiful place to enjoy a long, quiet, and sunny walk surrounded by radiant ocean views. It is an amazing location to live an aquatic adventure in a kayak, paddle board or small boat. Many nice access points can be found around the bay at small ocean parks and parking lots. One of the best known and easily accessible locations is at Saanichton Bay Park. In addition, you can head out to discover so many unique points of view along the bay. These give you a wonderful feeling of traveling far from the center of the city without having to go to far. It has a very calm and warm atmosphere that surrounds you, making it ideal for relaxing.

DAY

13

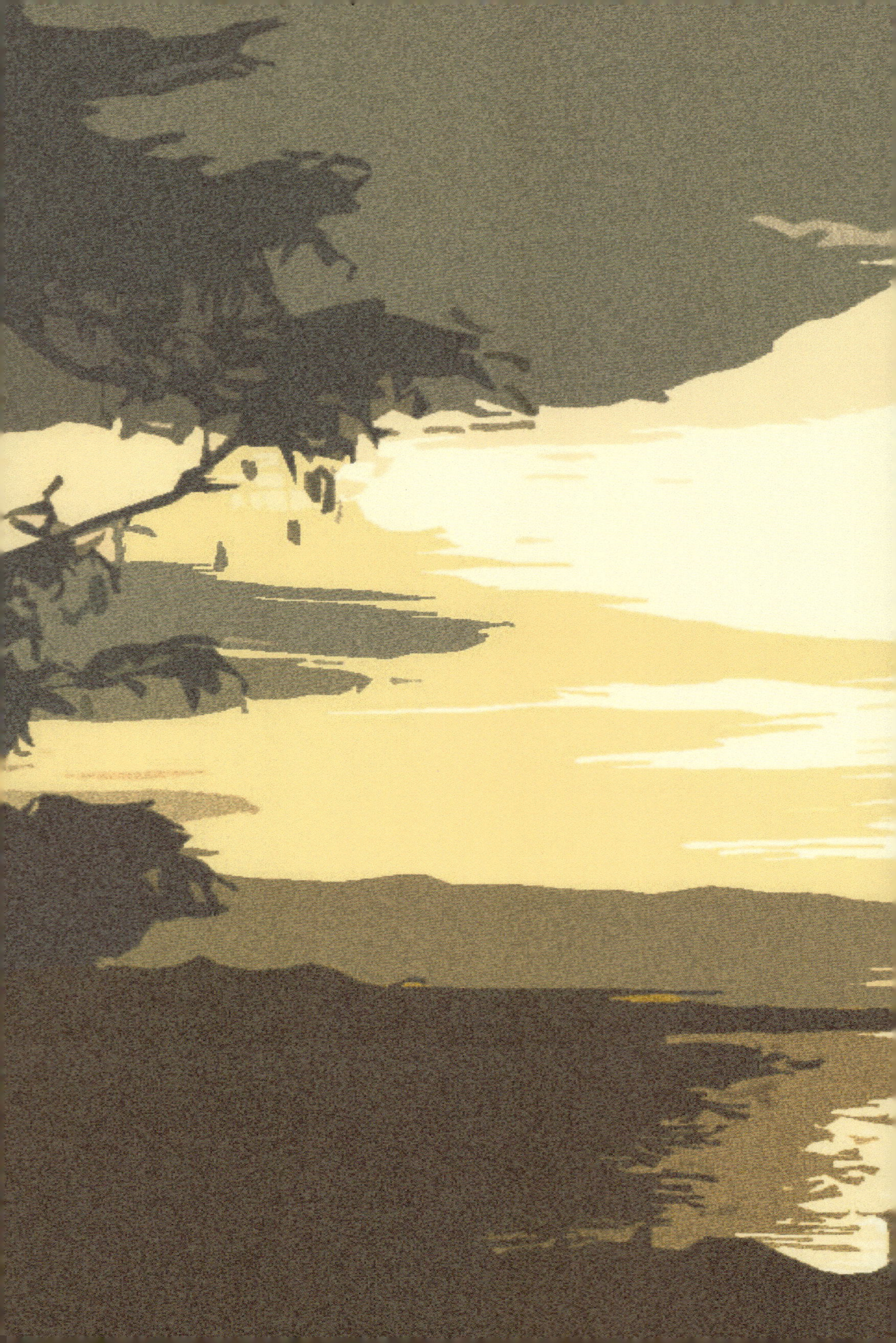

OCEAN SIDE

16

A LITTLE ROSS BAY BEACH

IDEAL TIME
30 MIN
DAY

Little Ross Bay Beach is a beautiful spot at the end of Dallas Road that is covered with some small rocks and a few logs. It is a little and calm beach which makes it ideal for reading a book or admiring the landscape. While the wind and waves can be strong at times, it is still a good spot for a quick dip in the ocean, especially when the sun is shining. You can also go kayaking or paddle boarding, or simply go for a short stroll at sunset. Sometimes, with a bit of luck, you can see some otters or seals in the vast horizon. What stands out the most is this lovely view of the little ocean house on the edge of the beach with its amazing mountain landscape.

B PUBLIC BEACH ACCESS

**IDEAL TIME
20 MIN
DAY**

In the city of Victoria, as in all of the island, many small access points to the ocean can be found everywhere. Most access points are a staircase taking you directly to the edge of the ocean and sometimes, they aren't even found on a map. It is nice to appreciate a new viewpoint at each new location. These little destinations only have a few people who come visit at one time, which makes it perfect for time with you and your thoughts. It is awesome for a quick stop to take in the soft sound of the waves and birds while watching the view. It is ideal for reading a book or going for a short stroll in your day.

GONZALES BAY

**IDEAL TIME
1 – 2 HOURS
DAY/NIGHT**

C

Gonzales Bay has some of the best and simple walks in eastern Victoria to watch many incredible sunsets. The colors of the sunsets here change from yellow to golden and sometimes even to pink. All this while enjoying an unobstructed view of the ocean. It is a peaceful place to relax and enjoy a long walk surrounded by pretty houses and beaches. As you walk, you will come across Gonzales Park, a little sandy beach with a few logs and great views of the bay. Additionally, there is a small area on the beach that is surrounded by trees and picnic tables ideal for cooling off in the shade. It is a perfect place to swim or play in the sand.

D | **TRAFALGAR PARK** | **IDEAL TIME
30 MIN-1 HOUR
DAY/SUNSET**

Trafalgar park has a lovely walk to do at the end of Gonzales Bay. This park is different from a typical park because it has a walk on top of large rocks surrounded by nature and incredible views. The best viewpoint is at the beginning of the pretty little stone staircase in harmony with mother nature. Also, you will find a beautiful outstanding sculpture, the Winds of Time. Above all, you can come to see many breathtaking sunsets. At the bottom of the slope, you will find a small and calm beach that is great for relaxing while listening to the sound of the ocean and admiring the vast horizon.

E MCNEILL BAY

IDEAL TIME
30 MIN
DAY

McNeill Bay has a nice walk to enjoy the large and serene waterfront beaches and parks. On one end of the bay there is Sunny Lane Beach, a tiny beach with a natural arch at its entrance. This place is a nice location to start an adventure on a kayak. As you are walking on the edge of the bay, you will find many access points to the water. The entire bay is nice for kayaking and paddleboarding any time of the year. At the other end of the bay, you will find Haynes Park, a green space with benches and a stunning view of the ocean. At this park, on the left side, you will find a small access leading to a secluded, quiet, and sandy beach.

F

TURKEY HEAD WALKWAY

**IDEAL TIME
30 MIN
DAY/EVENING**

Turkey Head Walkway has a wonderful and peaceful little stroll at the edge of the water. It will surprise you with its endless panorama of the amazing sky and ocean. The trail is surrounded by lovely flowers and benches on one side and large rocks overlooking the vast ocean on the other. When you get to the end, you will find a stretch of beach with a long line of rocks that you can climb on and walk over to the Oak Bay Marina sign. There, you will have a chance to see some marine life, such as the giant jellyfish of the region. There is also a restaurant, café, gift shop, and a lot of boats to look at.

G ## CATTLE POINT

**IDEAL TIME
30 MIN-1 HOUR
DAY/SUNSET**

After Willows Beach you will find a set of stairs that will take you directly to the pretty Cattle Point trail surrounded by flowers and trees along the way. After a short walk, you will enjoy a breathtaking view of the ocean and an area around large flat rocks. From here, you can admire one of the most beautiful sunsets on the water's edge, making it an ideal place for a romantic picnic. If you wish to continue your walk, you will pass through an area of green grass with a few benches. Then you will come across Brody Bay which has a beach mainly covered by rocks and logs. It is ideal for watching birds, sea life, and waves dancing with the wind.

H FUNNEL COVE BEACH

IDEAL TIME
20 MIN
DAY

Funnel Cove Beach is a very quiet and uncrowded small beach. It is a good spot for a little picnic or immersing yourself in a good book. It is a great place to see the sun's reflection as it sparkles all across the ocean. On the way to this beach you will walk along an awesome path surrounded by trees and very green nature throughout the year. Once you arrive, the only background noise that you will hear are the songs of the birds. You can then continue your walk on the top of the large rocks to admire an even closer view of the landscape and for the bravest, enjoy a good refreshing dip in the water.

SPOON BAY BEACH

I

**IDEAL TIME
15 MIN
DAY**

Spoon Bay Beach is a very small beach that is on top of large rocks overlooking a unique landscape. It has an outstanding background with a lovely little island protruding from the water. There, you can have a quick swim in the clear water at any time of the year even if it remains rather cold. It is a good place to go kayaking or enjoy a short break by the ocean with a chance to encounter some adorable marine life. This place may be small but it still gives the impression of flying over a vast ocean world. On a crazy sunny day, this place becomes an enchanting piece of paradise where you can enjoy a moment of tranquility.

J LOON BAY PARK / BEACH

**IDEAL TIME
15 MIN
DAY**

Loon Bay Park Beach is a wonderful place to enjoy the silence of nature with a peaceful view of the ocean and the Royal Yacht Club. One of its best assets is its magical staircase ending in a beautiful arch of natural leaves. It gives a nice feeling of crossing through to a wonderful paradise. On the other side of the arch is a cute sandy beach. The sand here is very different from other beaches because it gives a special impression that can not be explained. It is very soft and smooth. There is also a park surrounded by trees with a bench overlooking the harbor and its beautiful boats.

HIBBENS CLOSE BEACH ACCESS

K

**IDEAL TIME
20 MIN
DAY**

The access to the beach at the end of Hibbens Close starts with a nice wooden staircase that is surrounded by cute plants and flowers. It has a magnificent view of the ocean with one of those kinds of little beaches across the island that you won't find on many maps. It is a very discreet little beach that is like a gem found on your way. This beach has a mixture of sand and small rocks, and sometimes it is completely covered by water. It is a great place to swim or go for a walk barefoot all along the water. At the end of the beach, you will come across a beautiful and huge tree standing above the water with a handmade rope swing.

BAYNES BEACH

L

IDEAL TIME
30 MIN
DAY

Baynes Beach is a pleasant waterfront that has a surface made of rock where you will have an amazing feeling of being one with the ocean. At the entrance, a voluminous tree stands besides a small green area giving a warm welcoming sensation. After, on the rocks, you will find a great view of the ocean that is full of radiant energy. Be cautious because the waves can sometimes become very rough and hit the edge with a powerful force. This can make the beach very slippery and dangerous. You can go there for a revitalizing walk where you will see unobstructed views of the ocean and waterfront homes.

M TELEGRAPH COVE BEACH

**IDEAL TIME
20 MIN
DAY**

Telegraph Cove Beach has the same name as a really famous spot in the north of the island, so it can be confusing. This is a great beach on the east side of Victoria that is covered in small rocks. At the end of the beach is a strip of large rocks that is fun to explore. The wind is often very choppy and the waves often raging, so it is a wonderful place to admire the power of mother nature. It is a nice location to enjoy a very early sunset that melts from yellow to pink. Although the water can be very cold, this place is great for soaking your feet, enjoying a short walk along the water's edge, or simply relaxing and watching the view.

CRANFORD & GUINEVERE PARKS

N

IDEAL TIME
15 MIN
DAY

The parks of Cranford and Guinevere are two discreet little waterfront locations where your chances of being alone are high. You will find these spots through a series of very small streets. They are surrounded by various nature with an ocean that generally has a very strong temperament. It gives you a feeling of being out in the Canadian wilds with only being minutes from the city center. They both have magnificent viewpoints by the beach that are nice to admire during a short break in your afternoon. These places are adorable for a very short stroll, reading a good book, or even a short nap.

FINNERTY COVE BEACH

**IDEAL TIME
30 MIN
DAY**

Finnerty Cove beach begins with a short walk through a passage between the trees, leading straight to a large rocky area. This amazing beach has a surface made of rock and is generally very calm but it may also become very windy. It is a great place to catch some crabs while having various outstanding views. Along the path you will find a wooden patio on the edge of the beach where you can enjoy a moment of sheltered rest. Then, to complete the walk, there is a passage leading through a grove of trees to a pleasant neighborhood where you have a chance to come across some deer and squirrels.

HOLLYDENE PARK / BEACH

P

IDEAL TIME
30 MIN
DAY

Hollydene Park Beach is one of the loveliest little beaches in eastern Victoria. Very discreet, its entrance starts with a small path in the shade through a natural area. It leads straight to a staircase that gives access to a sumptuous beach covered with sand and small gravel. Along the entire beach, you can find many shells of all kinds and small sea creatures. Like some other beaches, it depends on the time and season, but can become completely covered by water, which gives it a whole new and wonderful charm. The beach ends on a rocky slope that is easy to climb where you can sit and watch the view or just continue on to the next beach.

GLENCOE COVE KWATSECH PARK

**IDEAL TIME
1 HOUR
DAY**

Glencoe Park is a big place to enjoy an amazing walk along the high edge of the water. You can find several dozens little passages that will bring you to a variety of beautiful viewpoints. As well, you will have a feeling of ocean freshness. At this park, you can go for a short or long walk depending on the paths you choose to take. If you choose to go up to the end, you will come across a little beach with a very different setting than the other spots in this park. You can choose to stop and relax on this beach or continue your little adventure along the water's edge on a strip of rocks. There, you will see even more beautiful and magical views.

R | TIMBER BEACH & D'ARCY LANE

**IDEAL TIME
20 MIN
DAY/SUNSET**

Timber Beach and D'arcy Lane are two unusual and pretty places that are as nice by day as by night. These unique spots are located just before the beginning of the charming Bay of Cordova. They are composed of long steel staircases which lead directly into the clear ocean water. This makes the water perfect for dipping your feet into. There are some large rock outcrops that surround these places which adds an exotic aspect to them. These are two great natural locations surrounded by the pleasant sounds of the water and a sublime ocean landscape where you may observe some seals swimming.

34

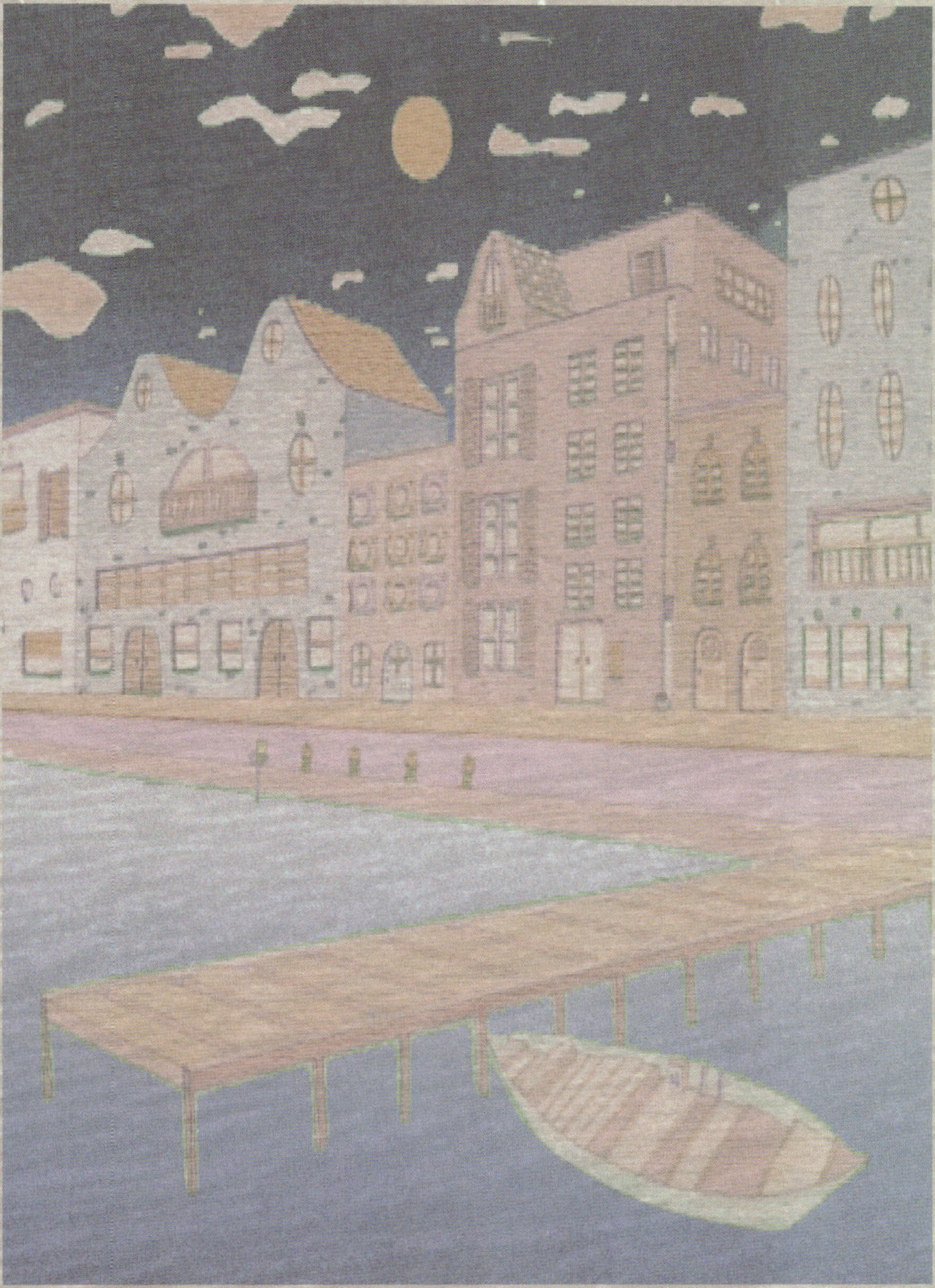

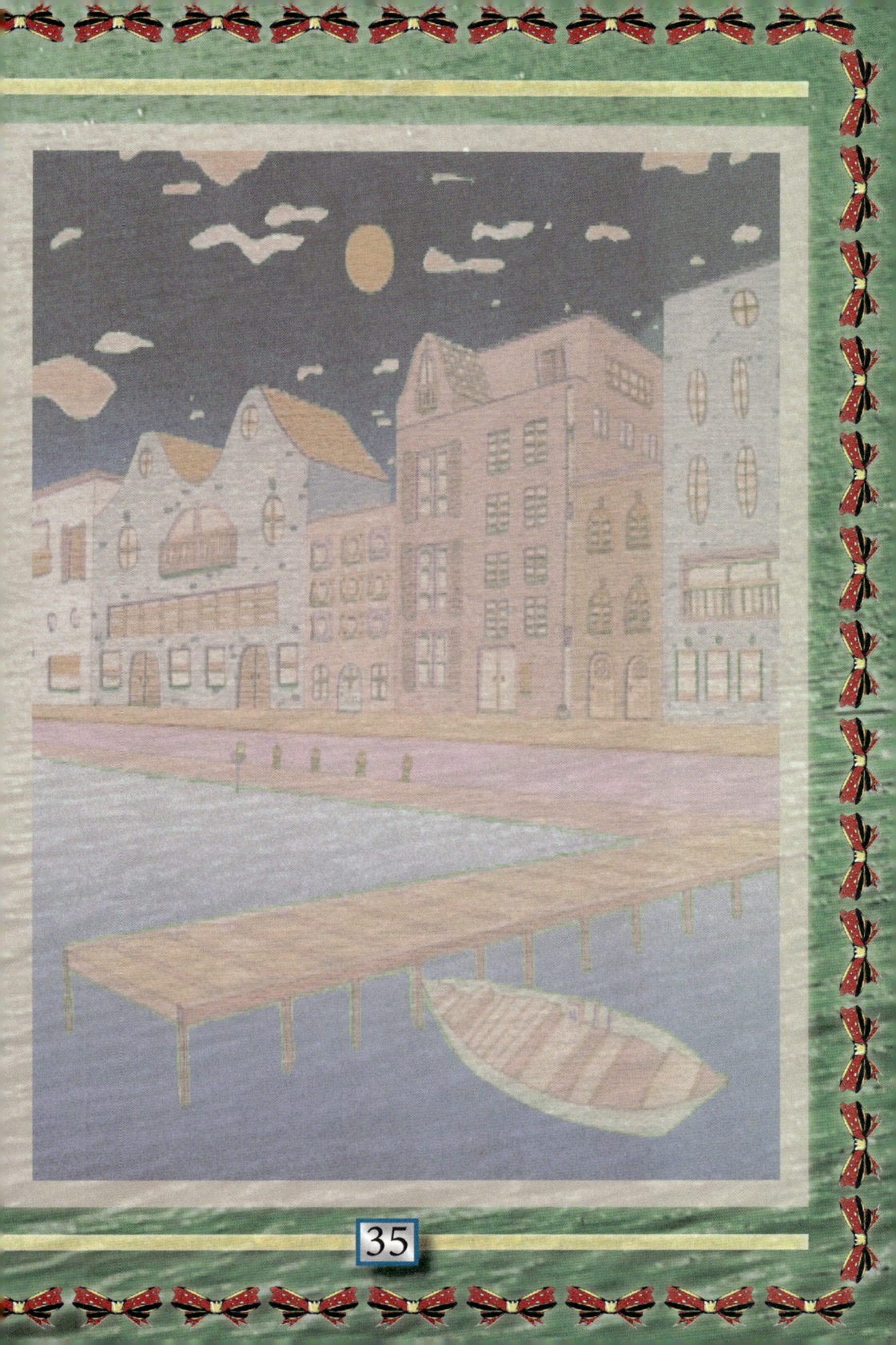

PARKS
& GARDENS

38

A ABKHAZI GARDEN

IDEAL TIME
30 MIN
DAY

The Abkhazi Garden has an elegant walk through beautiful trees and flowers all the way. Originally the home of Prince Nicolas and Princess Peggy of the Abkhazi family which has become a beautiful garden full of history and a variety of plants. It is a sensational destination that has an abundant of nature full of colors and smells which makes it very calming. You will find pretty little ponds with cute turtles chilling throughout the garden. The opening hours are different depending on the season, and the entry is by donation. Additionally, you can have lunch or a drink at the teahouse or check out the little souvenir shop.

39

B WALBRAN PARK

**IDEAL TIME
20 MIN
DAY/SUNSET**

Walbran Park offers scenic views from a historic World War II lookout. It is a very beautiful and simple park filled with small hills of rock and dry grass without any shade. At the top you can see a sublime viewpoint of a great large panorama of the ocean, mountains and urban landscape. It is nice to go to this place at the end of the day to watch a magical yellow/pink sunset. On the way, there is a path leading straight to the historic monument where you can learn more about the importance of the history and conservation of the beautiful area. Be cautious as the heat can be very strong here.

C GONZALES HILL

**IDEAL TIME
15 MIN
DAY/SUNSET**

At the end of Walbran Park, there is the Gonzales Hill. It has a glorious view to watch during a bright sunny day or a sunset when the wind is calm. You will enjoy a feeling of ocean freshness with its clear and expansive view from above the endless ocean and sky. From here, you can observe the whole view of Gonzales Bay with its lovely sandy beaches and houses. It is a small hill, easy to walk on, with benches, views, and the Gonzales Observatory standing beautifuly on the top of the big rocks of the hill. It was a weather station for 75 years and now it is a heritage building perched at the top of the hill giving a nice charm to the park.

D ANDERSON HILL PARK

IDEAL TIME
30 MIN-1 HOUR
DAY/SUNSET

Anderson Hill Park is an amazing place that begins with a few different passages in the midst of very generous vegetation. Surrounded by trees, flowers and dry grass, this natural walk will take you directly to its park. It has a large expanse of curved rocks in the ground giving hundreds of bumps all over which you can follow as you walk. From here, you will find gorgeous views of the ocean from eastern Victoria and its sunsets glinting on its waves. It is one of the most charming places for a picnic when the wind is calm and a perfect place to enjoy a sumptuous real Canadian landscape.

E BOWKER CREEK WALKWAY

**IDEAL TIME
30 MIN
DAY**

Bowker Creek Walkway is a lovely and fascinating walk that starts close to the Oak Bay Recreation Centre and passes through Oak Bay on the way to the ocean. It is a superb path which follows a long continuous stream of water that is usually filled with several ducks. There are many benches, bridges, and pretty colorful trees and flowers along the way. It is a calm and pleasant place to enjoy a jog or a walk during the beautiful sunshine of the city. Also, it is good to know that the Bowker Creek Initiative is a broad coalition working to protect and improve the ecological, social, and economic health of the Bowker Creek watershed.

F CARNARVON PARK

**IDEAL TIME
20 MIN-1 HOUR
DAY**

Carnarvon Park is a nicely developed sports park with many playing fields where you can play rugby, tennis, football, and many other sports. One of its best parts is that you can access the Rotary Water Park directly. Over there you can enjoy the fresh water while playing on the playground. Although the water park is very fun, use it at your own risk and supervision by an adult is advised. It is an ideal place to enjoy outdoor family activities on a hot summer day with picnic tables, washroom, and other accommodations. In Victoria, you can find other little water parks like this all over the city.

44

UPLAND PARK

G

**IDEAL TIME
30 MIN
DAY**

Uplands Park has many paths that are nice and easy to walk and explore with all its intersecting trails. This is a flat park that has an abundance of nature but is usually pretty dry and a little windy all year round. During your walk, you will find many rocky outcrops and a large grassy area for one of those cozy blanket picnics that you just can not resist on a warm sunny day. At the entrance, you will find a war memorial represented by a concrete sculpture of a woman standing and looking over the 97 names of Oak Bay's 1939-1945 war dead. It was crafted by Hames Saull and modeled after his wife.

MOUNT TOLMIE

H

**IDEAL TIME
40 MIN
DAY/SUNSET**

Mount Tolmie is a lovely park that is easily accessed and offers 360 degrees of amazing views of Victoria from the top. It has a natural meadow with exposed rock surfaces and several small gravel pathways which loop throughout the park. This place has plenty of picnic tables and it is nice to visit during a sumptuous sunny day or a lovley sunset. You can drive directly to the top to enjoy one of the greatest viewpoints it has to offer without having to do the hike. While the hike here is relatively easy compared to most mountainous hikes, there are still several steeper sections throughout the way.

46

I CEDAR HILL PARK

IDEAL TIME
1 HOUR
DAY

Cedar Hill Park surrounds the Cedar Hill Golf Course with a nice woodchip trail. This place has a very lovely boardwalk that does a long loop around the course. It passes through some little woods, King's Pond, and the Bowker stream where you will have the pleasure of seeing plenty of ducks. Generally considered as an easy route, it still takes an average of one hour to complete. It is a popular route for running, walking, and other outdoor activities. Also, this park is home to a variety of native and exotic wild animals and plants that you can discover during your walk. Be cautious as it is easy to walk into the golf course which may interfere with someones game.

47

FINNERTY GARDEN

J

**IDEAL TIME
20 MIN
DAY**

Finnerty Garden is a public woodland garden located on the edge of the UVic campus. This garden is filled with beautiful flowers and trees full of colors, and has lovely smells all year round. There are some ponds and benches all along the pathways and it is a real pleasure to take a gentle stroll here, especially during the pretty blooming seasons. One of the parks most interesting features is the huge variety of plants it has, most have a label to indicate the name of the species and some information about them. Futhermore, its main characteristic is the important collection of Rhododendrons skillfully planted.

48

K MYSTIC VALE

**IDEAL TIME
20 MIN
DAY**

Mystic Vale is a great place to enjoy a wonderful long walk through the woods. This small forest is also on the edge of the UVic campus and is ideal during all weather conditions. You will be surrounded by a pleasant silence and many tall trees where you will have a wonderful feeling following its many paths. When the sun is beating down, it is the perfect time to go there and enjoy the sparkling shine of the sun slipping between the gaps of the trees which gives it a magical and enchanting look. It is also a great place to go jogging, enjoying a picnic under the shadows, or even just listening to the rain falling with its wonderful smell.

L PHYLLIS PARK

**IDEAL TIME
30 MIN-1 HOUR
DAY/SUNSET**

Phyllis Park is one of those spots where you can enjoy many breathtaking views of the ocean in the middle of a generous natural setting. It is great for a sublime walk that has passages between large rocks and trees. It has a wooden bridge, a stone staircase, and several spots on small patios where you can enjoy a lovely and short break while admiring incredible views. The walk in this park can be a little more tiring than most eastern parks due to its hill, but its beauty and originality will make you want to see it! Once up the hill you will come across a lovely neighbourhood with some deer.

50

KONUKSON PARK

M

IDEAL TIME
40 MIN
DAY

Konukson Park is a great woods that begins with a pretty entrance integrating you little by little under an abundance of graceful nature. The park is located in a splendid and very quiet neighbourhood where you have a chance to encounter some cute animals. This park is surrounded by many different kinds of trees which make it a perfect place to appreciate a pleasant walk in the shade. It forms a little loop and is considered as an easy hike that you can enjoy without any problems. It is nice to go either on a rainy day to have a exotic rainforest feeling or on a sunny day while the sun shines magically between the trees.

N HARO WOODS PARK

IDEAL TIME
30 MIN
DAY

Haro Woods is a mystical and enchanting protected area where you can enjoy a nice walk in any weather. It takes you on a nice loop route through one of the most relaxing urban forests in Saanich that remain. It is considered as an easy route that is ideal for a hike, jog, or bike ride on a sunny day. It is good to know that dogs are welcome but must be kept on a leash. You can go for a walk on the designated trail or an adventure through all the woods full of tall slim trees standing beautifully all year round. It is similar in beauty to Mystic Vale but is more open allowing more sunlight through.

52

BOW PARK

O

IDEAL TIME
30 MIN
DAY

Bow Park starts its walk on a very magical path covered by an abundance of nature that leads you into the park. This path is in fact the greatest charm of the place, as it is always full of greenery with a beautiful wild side. At the end of this pathway, you will arrive directly to the center of the park. Here, there are many benches in front of a small duck pond surrounded by yellow trees and many colourful flowers. There is no view or lookout as it is a densely wooded area which brings a lot of calm and peace. This place is perfect for relaxing, reading, and watching birds and other wildlife that the park has.

53

P

SWAN LAKE

**IDEAL TIME
30 MIN-1 HOUR
DAY**

Swan Lake has a wonderful walk with well maintained wooden paths, docks, and a floating bridge that crosses in the middle of the lake. One of its unique features is that it is minutes away from the city yet gives you a nice sensation of being far away in the country. You will find different plants, shrubs, and ducks along an easy flat walk. The park is a bird and plant sanctuary where you usually only meet friendly people just enjoying the peaceful nature. It is really nice to have an area that is a mixture of forest and lake at the same time. You can also enjoy splendid viewpoints and specific lookout views on the wooden paths.

BLENKINSOP LAKE

Q

**IDEAL TIME
20 MIN
DAY**

Blenkinsop Lake is a lovely place that features a walk along the wooden bridge on the Lochside Regional Trail that crosses the lake. It is one of the best spots in the east of Victoria to begin a biking adventure. Here, there are many inaccessible natural areas that makes the walk at the lake really short but offers beautiful views. The best view on the path is in the middle where you will see a statue standing in front. This view has many sweet lilypads all over the edge of the water with a really nice hilly landscape. There are many good bird-watching places from the trail and bridge and is nice to visit during the summer as its greenery thrives.

R

MOUNT DOUGLAS

IDEAL TIME
1 – 3 HOURS
DAY/SUNSET

Mount Douglas is one of the best and most famous parks in the east of Victoria. The top of the hill presents you with an amazing 360 degree panoramic view of its surroundings with the ocean in the background. It is a very nice spot to catch one of the gorgeous pink, purple, or golden sunsets of the city. This location has plenty of hiking trails full of trees and other greenery along with many forest creatures. You can spend hours exploring but be careful has you can become disorientated. All these breathtaking views can be experienced without needing to hike the hill as you can drive to the top.

57

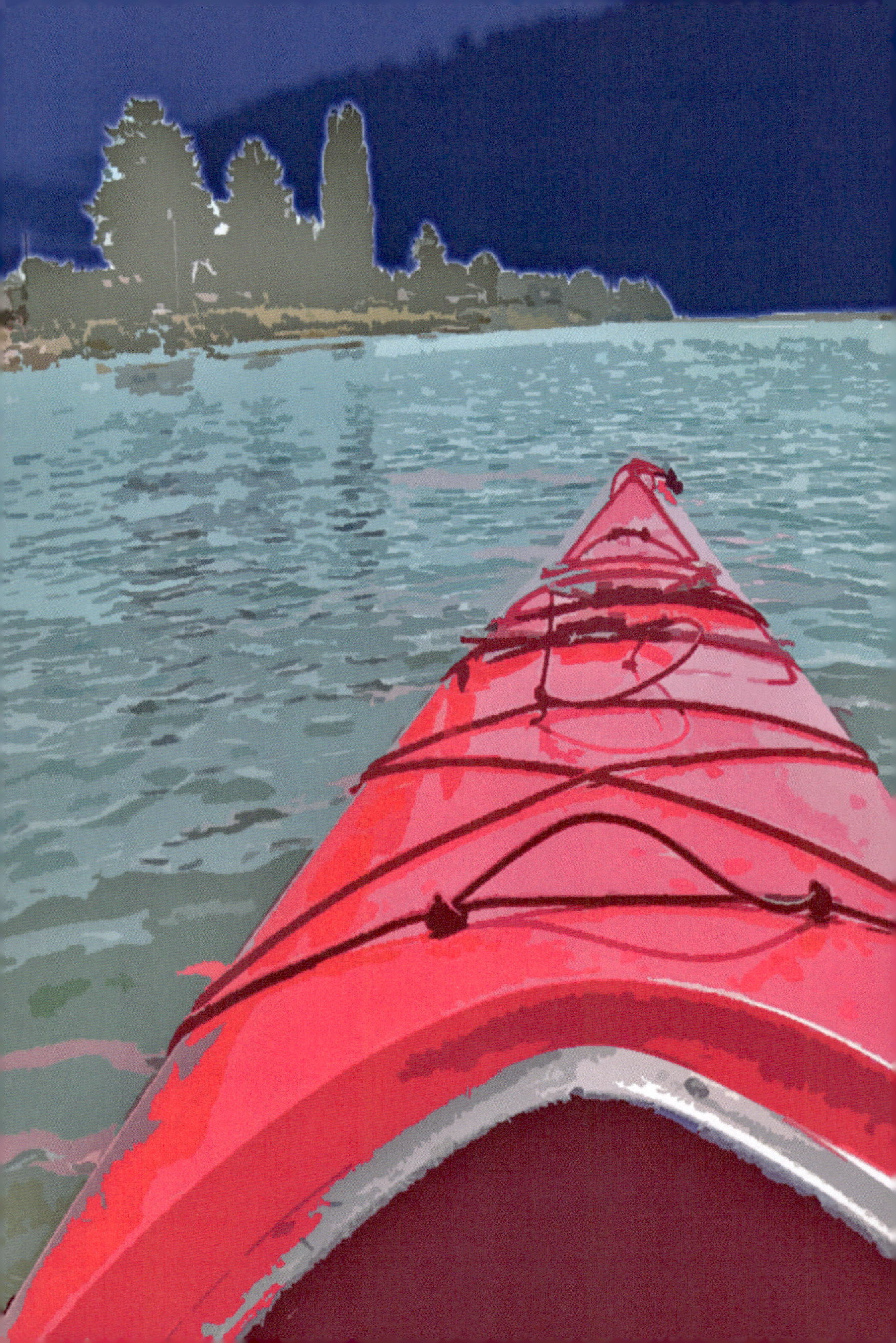

ACTIVITIES
& CULTURE

60

A UNIVERSITY OF VICTORIA (UVIC)

DAY/EVENING

The University of Victoria and its large surroundings are absolutely outstanding. It is a lovely location filled with a large abundance of nature full of various trees with several walks in the forests and parks. It is a nice place with dozens of little activities that you can find everywhere in the area like a little cinema (Cinecenta), theater (Phoenix), library, gym and large dormitories to accommodate all its students. Here, there are also a few small cafes and a pub/restaurant with several events throughout the year. It has a great mix of culture, technology, and nature throughout its entire grounds.

B ICE SKATING & HOCKEY

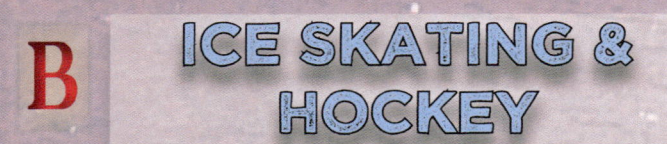

DAY/EVENING

It is well known that sports like ice-skating and hockey are popular in Canada. In the east of Victoria, you will find the fantastic Oak Bay Rec Center where you can enjoy these activities. Here, you can go on the iceskating rink for a simple skate with friends and family or take your equipment to play a game of hockey. It is open day and night but it is good to know that the designated times for skating or playing hockey vary according to the season. You can find this information online or pick up a brochure from the front desk to choose the ideal time to come and enjoy the activity of your choice.

C REC CENTERS & SPAS

DAY/EVENING

Like ice-skating and hockey in Canada, the gymnasiums and swimming pools are very popular. Usually, you will find them in every rec center accompanied by a sauna, steam room, and jacuzzi which makes these places perfect for having a fun afternoon or evening. Here, you can have the opportunity to relax all day or doing as much sport as you like. You can also find so many common activities in these pools such as aquafit, water slides, climbing, ropes, and so much more. Of course, these activities vary by recreation center and in the east of Victoria, there are Oak Bay Rec Center, Gordon Head, and Henderson to name a few.

D | CAFES, TEAS & GELATOS | DAY

The east of Victoria is full of very pretty and little places where you can have a delightful and local coffee or english tea. To the east delimited by the map, you can choose to go try the famous afternoon tea at Abkhazi Garden, Willows Beach, Oak Restaurant, and so many others. If you are more into coffee, then you will have even more choices to stop and discover lots of original places like the Demitasse Cafe & Garden. There is also many great places to eat some delicious ice cream or pastries. For ice cream, you can go to Marina Dockside Eatery next to a walk on the water's edge.

E RESTAURANTS & PUBS

DAY/NIGHT

To the east of Victoria you will find several restaurants and pubs where you can go and taste some very good and varied cuisines from around the world. They generally come up with a generous choice of original cocktails and local beers. Two good locations to go enjoy a romantic dinner by the water while watching a sumptuous sunset are the Marina Restaurant further south and the Beach House restaurant further north. You can also find any local breakfast spots which are really popular in Canada to enjoy some delicious pancakes and eggs Benedict for brunch. The Shine Café is a must try spot that you won't want to miss.

F SHOPPING CENTERS

DAY

Although being a capital, the city of Victoria does not have any major shopping malls like Metrotown in Vancouver. It is still really nice to go shopping for an afternoon in the few malls that you can find in the east. You can shop for fashion, merchandise, gifts, souvenirs, jewelry, flowers, chocolate, and so many other must haves at these places. Mayfair is the largest shopping center in the city which has a large food court with various foods and drinks. You can also try other smaller shopping centers such as the Hillside Shopping Center and the Broadmead Village Shopping Center.

G UPTOWN AREA

DAY

Uptown has a large cluster of shops of every kind with art spaces, patisseries, cafés, restaurants and so much more. It is an ideal place to admire during any season between its hundred lights and big Christmas tree during the winter, to its dozens of lovely cherry blossoms for the arrival of spring, to its thousands of colorful flowers in the summer, and do not forget the splendid colorful trees of autumn. Its most charming place is in the center, where you will find small water jets, a little cabana, and a bakery surrounded by beautiful trees. You can relax at a table under the sun or in a sweet little cabana sheltered from the wind and rain.

H OAK BAY AVENUE DAY

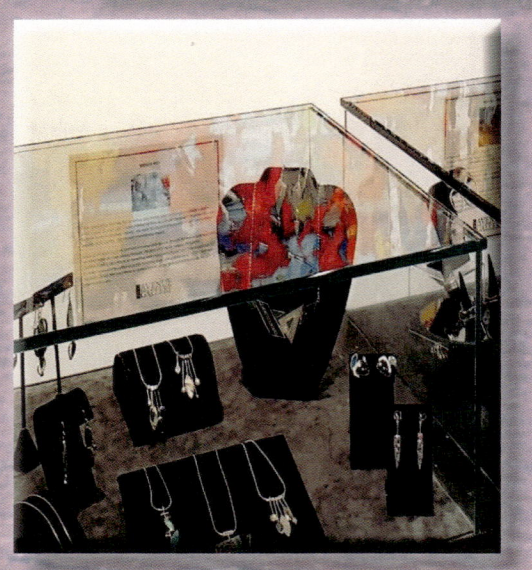

The Oak Bay Avenue is a lovely and large area where you will find many varieties of nice shops with a well maintained walk next to little parks and flowers. Here, you will find what ever you may need between restaurants, bakeries, coffee shops, tea houses, galleries, studios, art, flowers, jewelry, and so much more. You can also come to watch one of the city's parades throughout the year, like the 'tea parade' during the spring or the 'lighted trucks parade' during Christmas time. Even though it is an avenue near downtown, it is not noisy at all and you will even feel a very calming and relaxing feeling.

4 CATS ART STUDIO

I

DAY/EVENING

4cats is a great art studio where you can come and create your own artwork at your own pace with help if you may need. Almost all ages can participate and you can go on your own or with family and friends. There is something for everyone between projects with paint, polymer clay, or stoneware clay that can be done in a course or in a workshop, as well as several other special events. It is an awesome place to have fun through an activity that lets your imagination and artistic side run wild while having everything you need and step-by-step instructions for the project of your choice.

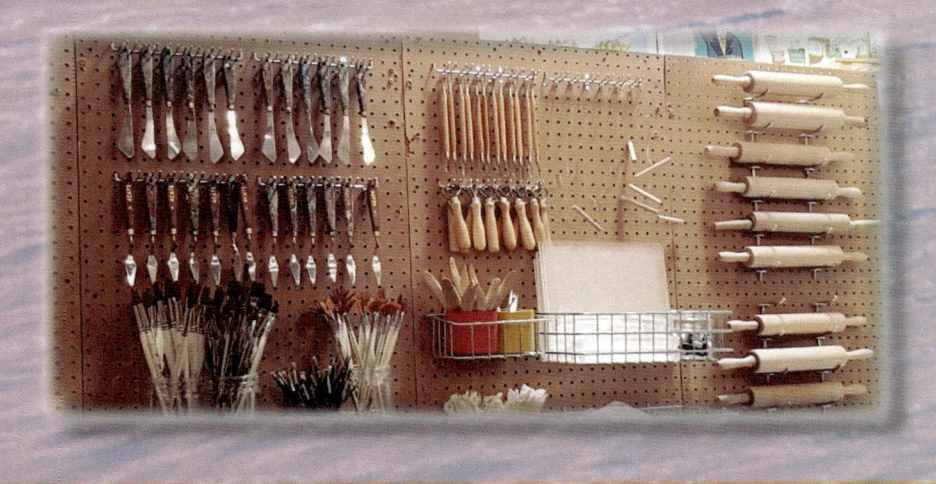

J # ARTS ALIVE OAK BAY

DAY/EVENING

Arts Alive is the Oak Bay Parks, Rec and Culture's annual public art program that exhibits stunning and original outdoor sculptures. New sculptures are selected each year by a jury and municipal audience to be borrowed from the artists. You can find them all over the neighbourhood of Oak Bay within the parks or along the streets. They are easy to find if you use the map on the Arts Alive site. Every year, there are new sculptures that are added to the collection. Oak Bay has built a permanent legacy of public art within its community with its very nice initiative to show art.

70

K — OAK BAY BEACH HOTEL SPA & POOL

DAY/EVENING

The Oak Bay Beach Hotel is a stunning building with an exsquisite entrance and a luxurious interior. This hotel offers a very unique activity that is its superb outdoor heated mineral pool accompanied by an incredibly spectacular view of the ocean. Access to its amazing heated swimming pool is only available for hotel or spa guests, which makes this a more pricey activity but can be an amazing and relaxing experience. Although the price is not easy, this activity remains one of the jewels of eastern Victoria to take full advantage of the ocean view while swimming in the warm water of the pool or relaxing all day without any worries.

KAYAKING & PADDLING

L

DAY

Two very popular activities in east Victoria are kayaking and paddle boarding. You should know that you have to be very careful with the current and the wind, which can be very strong. It is therefore advisable to go there on very calm days, when the conditions are ideal. This part of the ocean presents you with a magical adventure with its vibrant population of marine life, shores, islands, and heavenly coves. You will see locals doing these activities all year round and if you do not have gear, you can rent from 'South Island SUPs' or 'A day in Victoria SUPs' by the water's edge around Oak Bay.

M BIKING & HORSE BACK RIDING

DAY

In Victoria east, there is an equestrian facility named Valle Vista Stables, where you can enjoy a calm and amazing horseback ride. Here, you will get a warm welcome and a great ride that can be enjoyed all year round at a reasonable price. It is perfect for a great outdoor experience with many animals while having a great time. When it comes to biking, the east of Victoria is one of the best places around to cycle all year round. There are dozens of lanes and trails to explore the city and most importantly, a spectacular and scenic oceanfront bike path that stretches along Beach Drive. If you do not have a bike, then you can rent one and even try a tandem bike from Oak Bay Bicycles.

73

N TENNIS & GOLF

DAY

The east of Victoria has a lot of golf clubs and tennis courts which are generally surrounded by amazing and generous nature. These are very common sports for the people of Victoria. There are many clubs you can join with friends or family to play any day of the year. When it comes to game of tennis, it is better to have your own equipment and then choose the best court that suits you among a large quantity of free courts. When it comes to golf, the region is very popular with many different large courses available to regulars and visitors alike, as well as many deer for extra entertainment.

74

CITY PARKS

O

DAY

The city of Victoria is full of many municipal parks of all sizes where you can find various fun playgrounds for children to enjoy. One such place is Cadboro beach park with its giant sea monsters, another with its fun water jet park to cool off is the Carnavon park. These parks are generally accompanied by several picnic tables and public washrooms, and a large grassy area where you practice different sports and physical activities. It is also a really nice place to relax with a good book while sitting on the fresh grass. You will also see lots of pretty flowers and small animals around the various trees.

75

P AUTUMN WINTER WALK

DAY/EVENING

Over the Winter, for the spirit of Christmas, the city is lit up with millions of beautiful lights all over the trees, shops and throughout all the streets. These lights bring a magical and warm feeling everywhere in the east with its colorful and shiny decorations, events, and parades. Victoria is filled with so many unique trees that makes the experience of walking through the city during this period so enjoyable. In autumn, the city becomes one of the most magical places in the world with all the colors of the trees which bring it to life. Also, all streets and parks are covered with yellow, orange, and red trees and lovely new flowers.

Q   SPRING SUMMER WALK   DAY

Every year, Victoria city becomes an amazing place, especially for the arrival of the spring and summer flowers. Each has its own set of sweet flowers that bloom beautifully into a paradise of sensational smells and colors. Every season provides a radically changing experience but spring and summer are the best times to see the most abundant blooms. All over the parks and the streets, there are a lot of Wood Rose and Fuchsia Magellanica that are known as the dancing flowers. Specific to spring, there are the incredible and famous cherry blossoms all over the streets as well as Rhododendrons during parts of the summer.

WILDLIFE & SEALIFE

R DAY/EVENING

Victoria has a large diversity of animals that enjoy their lives in the gardens, lakes, beaches, and streets of the east of Victoria. The deers, squirrels, and seagulls are the most likely to be seen, but bunnies, raccoons, and eagles are seen quite often as well. They are treated with respect and given freedom by the inhabitants. When it comes to the sea creatures of the North-East Pacific Ocean you will find so many different and absolutely incredible species! The most common to be seen are otters, blue herons, seals, starfish, crabs and if you can travel by boat you may see some orcas, whales, or sealions.

79

© Edition Travel Victoria BC
'Victoria East', 2022
Victoria, Vancouver Island
British Columbia, Canada

Printing History: 1st Edition - 2022
Printed on demand by Amazon
Collection directed, illustrated and designed
by © Rose Dollsweet

Manuscript Proofreaders
Penelope Rokeby
Braydon Berthelet

CONTACT

www.travelvictoriabc.ca
@ Rose.design@outlook.fr
Travel Victoria BC
@Rose_dollsweet
@travelvictoria

Cataloging data available from the Library and Archives of Canada,
June 2022.

THE END

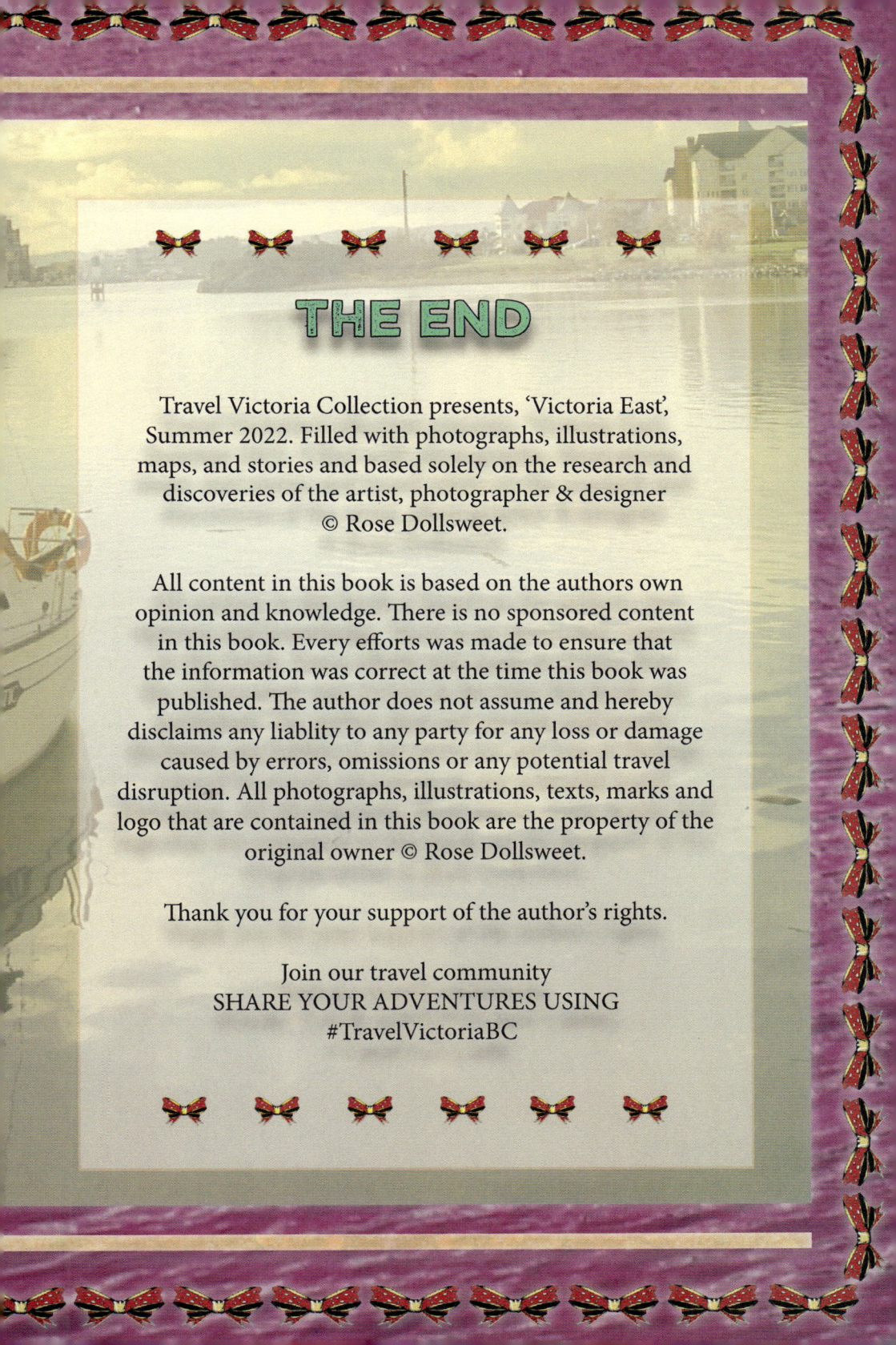

Travel Victoria Collection presents, 'Victoria East', Summer 2022. Filled with photographs, illustrations, maps, and stories and based solely on the research and discoveries of the artist, photographer & designer © Rose Dollsweet.

All content in this book is based on the authors own opinion and knowledge. There is no sponsored content in this book. Every efforts was made to ensure that the information was correct at the time this book was published. The author does not assume and hereby disclaims any liablity to any party for any loss or damage caused by errors, omissions or any potential travel disruption. All photographs, illustrations, texts, marks and logo that are contained in this book are the property of the original owner © Rose Dollsweet.

Thank you for your support of the author's rights.

Join our travel community
SHARE YOUR ADVENTURES USING
#TravelVictoriaBC

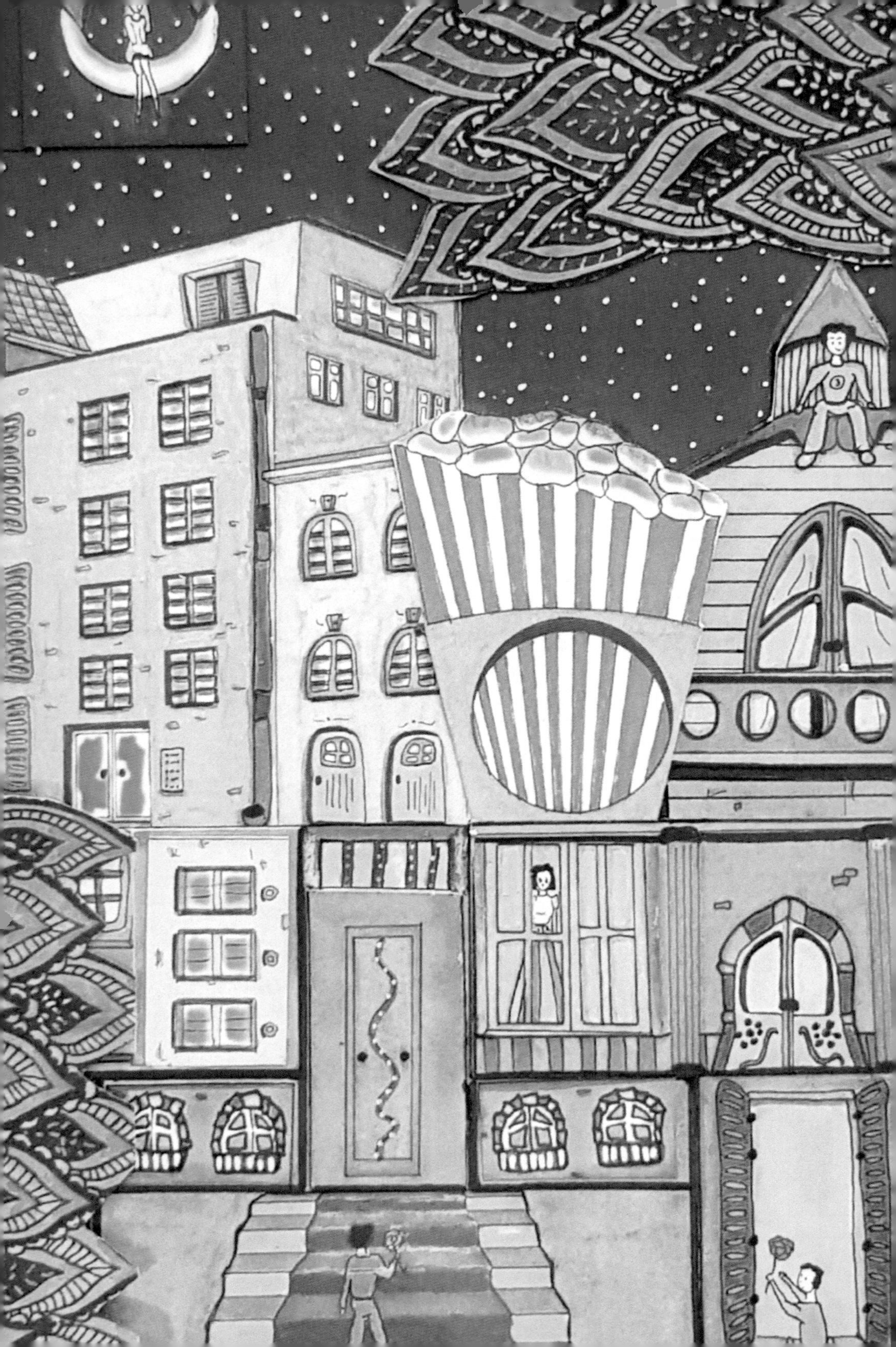

Printed in Great Britain
by Amazon